RABBITS, HATS AND SECRETS

STARRING DANE CERTIFICATE

Kirsty Hamilton

OXFORD
UNIVERSITY PRESS

OXFORD
UNIVERSITY PRESS

Great Clarendon Street, Oxford, OX2 6DP, United Kingdom

Oxford University Press is a department of the University of Oxford. It furthers the University's objective of excellence in research, scholarship, and education by publishing worldwide. Oxford is a registered trade mark of Oxford University Press in the UK and in certain other countries

British Library Cataloguing in Publication Data
Data available

ISBN: 978-0-19-830813-3

10 9 8 7 6 5 4

Paper used in the production of this book is a natural, recyclable product made from wood grown in sustainable forests. The manufacturing process conforms to the environmental regulations of the country of origin.

Printed in China by Golden Cup

Acknowledgements

Series Editor: Nikki Gamble
Cover photos: Fabrik Studios; Hurst Photo

Photography by Lindsay Edwards

The publishers would like to thank the following for the permission to reproduce photographs: **(bird perch)**: Margo Harrison/Shutterstock; **p7 (belt)**: Elnur/Shutterstock; **p8 (coins)**: Dibrova/Shutterstock; **p11b**: M. Unal Ozmen/ Shutterstock; **background images** by Jocic/Shutterstock; Scottchan/Shutterstock; Subbotina Anna/Shutterstock; Yganko/ Shutterstock; Yoolarts/Shutterstock; Saiva/Shutterstock; Natali Zakharova/Shutterstock; B. Melo/Shutterstock; LiliGraphie/ Shutterstock; Stocksnapper/Shutterstock

With thanks to Dane and Scarlett

CONTENTS

AMAZING ILLUSIONS

Do you ever dream of being able to perform **illusions**? As a young boy, this was my dream. I'm Dane Certificate — and I'm an illusionist!

One day I saw an amazing illusion being performed. The illusionist made sponge balls disappear into someone's hand! I decided I wanted to learn tricks like that.

Today, I perform all kinds of tricks in my **mysterious** show. Kids love coming to see me perform. Sometimes they get to be in the show, too.

Quick hands

One of the first tricks Dane learned was how to use his fingers very quickly to secretly hide and **reveal** things.

A SECRET COSTUME

For my shows, I wear a special costume. My costume looks simple but it has lots of hidden secrets.

bow tie
can spin around unexpectedly

inside pockets
perfect for hiding things quickly

bird perch
where my dove waits until I need him for a trick

top hat
for my 'rabbit in a hat' trick

sleeves
great for hiding things

outside pockets
easy to reach to pull
things out

belt
with hooks at the
back for secret items

7

PROPS

Many of my tricks include **props**. On stage, there is a red and black table with an old-fashioned suitcase on top. Inside the case are many different props.

handkerchiefs
I use these to hide and reveal things.

wand

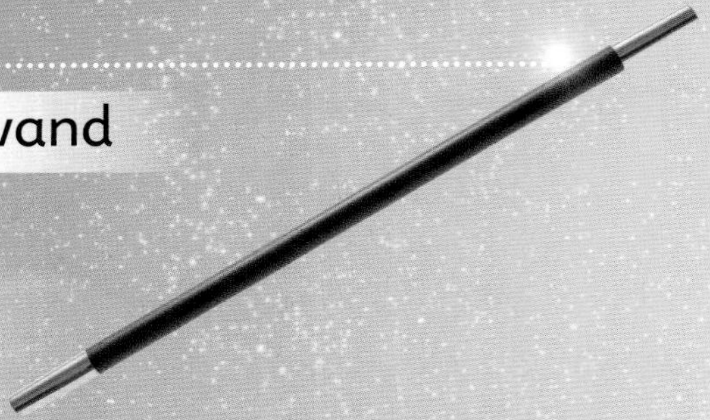

coins

linked rings

I slowly move these rings past each other and suddenly, they are linked!

sponge balls

trick flowers

cards

I use cards for mind-reading tricks.

ANIMAL STARS

Some amazing animals appear in my tricks. They have special training to make sure they stay safe.

Jack the rabbit is the star of my 'rabbit in a hat' trick. Here's what happens:

1. I show the audience the empty top hat.
2. I wave my wand over the hat.
3. Suddenly Jack pops out of the hat!

I also have a white dove called Ice Cream. In one of my tricks, I make him appear suddenly in my hands.

Creamy feathers

Ice Cream was named by a boy who came to my show. He thought the dove's white feathers looked like vanilla ice cream!

GETTING TRICKY

Here are a few tricks you can try for yourself.

TRICK 1: ICED WATER

YOU WILL NEED:

- a sponge
- a cup
- ice cubes
- a jug of water.

PREPARATION

1. Stuff the sponge tightly into the bottom of the cup.

2. Place two ice cubes on top of the sponge.

1. Pour a small amount of water into the cup (the sponge will soak it up).

2. Turn the cup upside down. Amaze your audience as two ice cubes fall out!

TRICK 2: SAWING SOMEONE IN HALF

YOU WILL NEED:

- an envelope
- scissors
- a marker pen
- a piece of paper that is narrower and longer than the envelope.

PREPARATION

1. Seal the envelope, cut off the ends and push gently on the creases to make a tube.

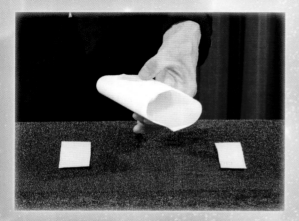

2. Flatten the tube and cut two slits in the back of the envelope almost up to the crease.

3. Draw a person on the paper, with the head at one end and the feet at the other.

PERFORMANCE

1. Flatten your envelope and slide the paper person into the envelope, up through the first slit and under the second slit. Only show the audience the front of the envelope.

3. Pull the paper person out of the envelope. Show the audience that the person is still in one piece!

2. Cut the envelope in half but make sure you only cut in front of the person.

HELPING HAND

To help me with my shows, I have a brilliant **apprentice** called Scarlett.

It's always busy being an apprentice. I make sure all the right props are on stage for each trick and hand them to Dane when he needs them. I also make sure the lights and music come on at the right times during the show.

Amazing apprentice tips

- Practise your part in the show until it's perfect.

- Organize the props so they are in the right order for the tricks.

- Wear a sparkly hat or a brightly coloured piece of clothing.

- Smile, be confident and look at the audience.

SPECIAL EFFECTS

Special effects are a great way of creating an **atmosphere** of mystery in a show.

MUSIC

First I play the piano and make a melody. Next, I write the words and record the song. Finally, I put it together with my tricks.

LIGHTS

If I'm doing a **dramatic** trick, I might use flashing lights. I use coloured lights, too. Blue lights can make people feel cold. Red lights can make them feel hot!

VIDEO

I also **project** video images across the stage, using my computer. These might be stars or patterns.

Dry ice

I use **dry ice** to create clouds of white smoke inside my theatre. This adds a feeling of mystery.

PLANNING A SHOW

When it's time to plan a new show, Scarlett and I talk about our ideas. We make a list of tricks and put them in order. We make sure there is a great opening and closing trick.

REHEARSALS

We **rehearse** each trick over and over again. The tricks need to be perfect before they can be performed to an audience.

SHOW TIME!

At last, it's show time! Scarlett and I have practised hard. We have everything ready. Soon the audience begins to arrive. Everyone is excited!

Battling nerves

It's natural to feel nervous before a show. Take a deep breath and smile. You will be brilliant!

Music begins to play and the theatre fills with mysterious smoke. Suddenly, the lights start flashing. The curtains are drawn back. "I am Dane Certificate," I say, "welcome to my show!" I open the suitcase of props and reach inside …

WHICH TRICK WOULD YOU LIKE TO SEE FIRST?

Taking a bow

At the end of a show, always take a bow.

GLOSSARY

apprentice: a person who is learning from someone with more experience

atmosphere: a feeling around you

dramatic: something sudden that gets your attention

dry ice: a special gas that can be made solid. When dry ice is put in water, it makes clouds of fog and smoke.

illusions: things that appear to be happening, but are not

mysterious: strange or difficult to understand

project: display pictures on a flat object such as a screen or wall

props: things that are needed for a performance

rehearse: practise

reveal: show something that has been hidden

INDEX